A Declaration by the Representatives of the UNITED STATES OF AMERICA in General Congress assembled.

When in the course of human events it becomes necessary for one people to dissolve the political bands which have connected them with another, and to assume among the powers of the earth the separate and equal station to which the laws of nature & of nature's god entitle them, a decent respect to the opinions of mankind requires that they should declare the causes which impel them to the separation.

We hold these truths to be self evident; that all men are created equal; that they are endowed by their Creator with inherent & inalienable rights; that among these are life, liberty & the pursuit of happiness; that to secure these rights governments are instituted among men, deriving their just powers from the consent of the governed; that whenever any form of government becomes destructive of these ends, it is the right of the people to alter or to abolish it, and to institute new government, laying it's foundation on such principles & organising it's powers in such form as to them shall seem most li

A Crowell Holiday Book

The

Fourth of July

BY MARY KAY PHELAN

Illustrations by Symeon Shimin

Thomas Y. Crowell Company, New York

CROWELL HOLIDAY BOOKS
Edited by Susan Bartlett Weber

2   3   4   5   6   7   8   9   10

The
Fourth
of
July

A birthday is a very special day. Every boy and girl celebrates a birthday once a year.

But in the United States we celebrate another birthday, too. It is called the FOURTH OF JULY. It is the birthday of our nation.

Our country has not always been a big and busy nation. Long ago the wide prairies and thick forests, the high mountains and winding rivers were here. But there were no farms, no towns, no cities. And the only people were the Indians.

Columbus discovered America in 1492. But it was many years before people from Europe came to live in the new land. The first settlers came from England. Most of them lived along the east coast.

By 1750 there were thirteen small colonies. Each colony was like a separate little country. However, they all were ruled by the king of England.

As the years passed, men began asking each other why they should be ruled by a king who lived across the ocean. They did not like sending taxes to England. They wished to be free to choose the kind of government they wanted.

Almost every village had a large Liberty Tree with wide-spreading branches. Men met under them to talk about freedom.

But the king of England refused to give up his American colonies. He sent ships filled with soldiers to the city of Boston. He was ready to start a war.

The colonies could no longer act as thirteen separate little countries. If they wanted independence, they knew they must work together.

The people in every colony, except Georgia, chose several men to go to Philadelphia and meet together. This group of men was called the "First Continental Congress."

For many days there was much talk at this First Continental Congress. Finally the men decided to send a letter to King George III. They asked him to order his soldiers back to England. They also asked him to change the unfair laws he had made.

King George III answered the colonists by sending more soldiers to Boston.

Now the colonists knew they would have to fight if they wanted to be free.

Again the members of Congress hurried to Philadelphia. They chose a leader for the army. He was tall, handsome George Washington.

Day after day the men from the colonies talked and talked. A few were still loyal to the king, but most men wanted to be independent.

Finally a brave decision was made. The thirteen colonies would unite as one country. They would call themselves the United States of America. They would tell the world they no longer belonged to England.

Five men were appointed to draw up this Declaration of Independence. Young Thomas Jefferson from Virginia was asked to write the words.

Night after night he worked at his desk. Mr. Jefferson wrote that "all men are created equal." He also wrote that everyone has a right to "life, liberty, and the pursuit of happiness." He said the people of the United States would choose the kind of government they wanted.

After Mr. Jefferson had finished, the Declaration was read to the Congress. The members liked the proud and honorable words which Thomas Jefferson had written.

On July 4, 1776, all Philadelphia was excited. Something important was about to happen. Early that morning a young boy hurried to the State House. If the men voted to adopt the Declaration of Independence, the boy wanted to signal the bell-ringer in the tower.

All day long the boy waited. As daylight began to fade, the final vote was taken. The Declaration of Independence was adopted.

When the boy heard the wonderful news, he shouted, "Ring, ring!" In the State House tower, the old bell-ringer began tugging at the bell rope. The ringing of the Liberty Bell told all Philadelphia that on this day—July 4, 1776—a new nation was born.

Four days later, the Liberty Bell rang again. It called the people of Philadelphia to the State House yard. They heard the Declaration of Independence read aloud for the first time. When the reading was finished, the people clapped and shouted.

A copy of the Declaration was sent to General George Washington in New York City. When it was read to the American soldiers, everyone cheered. Now they knew they were fighting for the freedom of their own country.

Bonfires were lighted. Guns were fired. Some soldiers even pulled down a statue of King George III. The lead, they said, could be melted and made into bullets for American guns.

When the news reached Boston, the people were overjoyed. They ran shouting through the streets. The American soldiers fired their cannon thirteen times to honor the thirteen new American states.

On and on the news traveled. Men on horseback carried copies of the Declaration in their saddlebags. They rode hundreds of miles over the mountains and through the valleys, taking the wonderful news to every part of America.

Finally one of the riders reached a village in South Carolina. Few people there knew how to read. But nine-year-old Andrew Jackson had been reading since he was five. He was asked to read the Declaration of Independence to the people in the village square. This freckle-faced boy later became the seventh President of the United States.

One year later the idea of celebrating the birthday of our nation began in Philadelphia. On July 4, 1777, bells once again rang out across the city. Bonfires blazed against the night sky. Many people placed lighted candles in their windows.

Four more years passed before the war against England was won. But even during these years, Americans celebrated each Fourth of July. Often they gathered under the Liberty Tree to listen to the reading of the Declaration of Independence.

After the War for Independence had ended, the Fourth of July celebrations grew bigger. Almost every town had a picnic. Tables were set up in the square, and everyone brought huge baskets of food.

There were sack races and watermelon-eating contests. Sometimes the boys tore around trying to catch a greased pig.

When the picnic was over, the band gave a concert. Everyone sang "Yankee Doodle."

Then came the speeches. Often a boy read the Declaration of Independence. And the day usually ended with the shooting of firecrackers.

As the years passed, people began planning special events for the Fourth of July. On July 4, 1817, ground was broken for the Erie Canal in Rome, New York. This was the first waterway to link the East with the West.

The Baltimore and Ohio Railroad was the first big railroad in our country. It was started in 1828. At a Fourth of July celebration Charles Carroll turned the first shovel of earth for this new railroad. Mr. Carroll was the only man still living who had signed the Declaration of Independence. He was ninety-one.

For many years people had wanted a way to honor George Washington, our first President. It was finally decided to build a monument in Washington, D.C. On July 4, 1848, the cornerstone was laid. There was a huge celebration.

Now each Fourth of July thousands of people watch the blaze of fireworks around the beautiful stone shaft.

The year 1876 marked the hundredth birthday of the United States. The people of Philadelphia were proud that the Declaration of Independence had been signed in their city. They decided to celebrate the birthday with a World's Fair.

In Ohio an artist, Archibald Willard, heard about the fair. He wanted to paint a picture for America's hundredth birthday. The picture, he decided, would show a boy, a father, and a grandfather marching off to fight in the war for freedom.

Mr. Willard asked thirteen-year-old Henry Devereux to pose as the drummer boy. When the painting was finished, people began calling it "The Spirit of '76." Before the fair was over, it became the most famous picture in America.

All America joined in celebrating the nation's hundredth birthday. Torchlight parades were held in every part of the country.

The biggest parade of all was in Philadelphia. Bells pealed, whistles blared, and bands played.

Thousands of people marched to the old State House in Independence Square. On the stroke of midnight a bell tolled thirteen times to honor the thirteen original states.

On July 4, 1884, the United States received a big birthday gift from the people of France. It was the Statue of Liberty.

In her left arm the statue held a book with "July 4, 1776" carved on the cover. The sculptor, Auguste Bartholdi, said this date would always remind the world of America's love for liberty.

Today you may visit this famous birthday gift. It is on an island in New York harbor.

On the Fourth of July we fly the American flag. For a long time there were forty-eight stars in the flag. Then on July 4, 1959, a new star was added. Alaska had become the forty-ninth state.

Exactly one year later, another star was added for Hawaii. Now we are a nation of fifty states with fifty stars in our flag.

Today the Fourth of July is celebrated in different ways. For more than one hundred years the people of Lititz, Pennsylvania, have held a "Fairyland of Candles."

At six in the morning church bells begin to chime. They celebrate the ringing of the Liberty Bell on that first Fourth of July. There is music all day long. As dusk falls, boys begin lighting ten thousand candles in a park. Everyone comes to see the play which the children present.

The birthday of our country is a big summer holiday for everyone. Almost every town has a celebration. Sometimes it starts with a long parade. Cub Scouts and Brownies march behind the band, waving flags.

After the parade there are soapbox derbies and swimming races. Often the Little League team in one town plays the Little League team from another town.

People everywhere have picnics. And after dark the boys and girls make circles in the air with their sparklers. Sometimes the grown-ups set off a fireworks display.

Many other countries, too, celebrate an Independence Day. In France it's called "Bastille Day" and comes on the fourteenth of July. Mexico has a "Festival of Independence" which lasts several days in September.

But Denmark is the only country that celebrates our Fourth of July. There it is called the "Rebildfest." People listen to songs and speeches about the friendship between the United States and Denmark.

The United States is one of the newest nations in the world. Yet our Fourth of July is one of the oldest of all Independence Days.

It's a day for parades and picnics, fireworks and fun. But it's also a day for remembering that first Fourth of July. We are proud of those patriots who signed the Declaration of Independence. They had the courage to make our country free.

About the Author

Mary Kay Phelan regards historical research as both a vocation and an avocation. She does research for and edits eight-millimeter historical movies. Her previous book in the Crowell Holiday series, *Mother's Day*, was begun in answer to a child's question about the holiday's origin. Mrs. Phelan felt that information on the Fourth of July was extremely important because many young children with whom she talked knew almost nothing about why Americans actually celebrate July 4.

Mrs. Phelan was born in Baldwin City, Kansas. She was graduated from DePauw University in Greencastle, Indiana, and received her M.A. from Northwestern University. She lives in Davenport, Iowa.

About the Illustrator

Symeon Shimin was born in Astrakhan, on the Caspian Sea, in Russia, and came to the United States with his family ten years later. He attended art classes at Cooper Union in the evenings. Mr. Shimin painted for a while in the studio of George Luks, but he is primarily self-taught and found his schooling for the most part in the museums and art galleries in this country and in France and Spain.

In 1938, Mr. Shimin was chosen to paint a mural in the Department of Justice Building in Washington, D.C. Recognition and many invitations to museum exhibitions followed, including those at the Whitney Museum of Art, the Art Institute of Chicago, the National Gallery in Washington, D.C., and the National Gallery in Ottawa, Canada. His paintings are in public and private collections.